the
architecture
of
eden

the
architecture
of
eden

eden project books

in association with
GRIMSHAW

Special photography by Edmund Sumner

foreword

SIR NICHOLAS GRIMSHAW

For me, the Eden Project starts at Paddington. Here we see an industrial structure built in 1854 with great innovative spirit by Brunel – who in turn was influenced by the famous greenhouse designer Sir Joseph Paxton. By coincidence, we were appointed to completely restore Paddington in the 1990s and Brunel's work and his attention to detail gave us a marvellous inspiration for our work in Cornwall.

Paddington will, of course, also be the start of many people's journey to Eden. From this wonderful structure, people will begin one of the finest train journeys in Europe. I think it is worth considering this journey and picking up some points that have affected us when working on our design.

Having cleared Reading, the train enters some of England's most spectacular countryside. Travelling the coast after Exeter in a southwesterly gale can mean that the sea actually throws itself over the train. Later, the train travels through the seaside town of Dawlish, inches from the seafront hotels and holidaymakers. It then passes over Brunel's famous Royal Albert Bridge at Saltash on the Tamar – another pioneering structure of great significance. Then onwards, clinging to hillsides where valleys open precipitously away from you, giving a spatial experience that is hard to repeat. After this are woods full of wild flowering rhododendrons, which seem to be unexplored and uncultivated by man.

Those visiting the Eden Project eventually arrive at St Austell and at this point one might ask why this immense botanical centre has been located here in Cornwall, in a lost valley that was previously a quarry. This question can be answered in several ways.

The first is climatic. Cornwall is the warmest part of the British Isles, so basing the project in a protected valley in the region gives considerable energy savings over other parts of the British Isles.

Another more intriguing answer is historical. The ports of Cornwall were the first landfalls encountered by many eighteenth- and nineteenth-century sea captains, many of whom collected plant specimens on their travels. Captain Cook was, of course, well known for his scientific interests – as was Sir Joseph Banks, the great eighteenth-century botanist. Ships' doctors in particular took great scientific interest in what they saw on their travels, and a large number of today's medicines originated from their early botanical finds. Many of these plant samples were 'dropped off' in Cornwall and found their way to the gardens of the great country houses of the time, one of which was Heligan.

The gardens of Heligan, since revived and restored under the direction of Tim Smit, can be viewed as the pilot study for the Eden Project. The gardens provide both year-round employment for substantial numbers of people in Cornwall and an extraordinarily successful tourist attraction.

This leads to the third major reason for the location of the Eden Project in Cornwall. A large number of people go to Cornwall for their holidays, so there is a substantial captive audience that welcomes an alternative attraction to the traditional day on the beach.

The combination of these locational factors, together with the British history of building greenhouses and wide-span structures, such as railway stations, makes it clear that one is bringing together two traditional British threads: an interest in plants and an interest in structures.

Following the completion of our International Terminal at Waterloo, which is one of the largest glazed structures in Europe, it may have seemed obvious that we should be selected as architects for one of the largest greenhouses in the world. However, the new structure is very different: the roof of Waterloo is, in environmental terms, a simple 'umbrella', whereas Eden's skin provides a controlled environment, with a vast range of temperatures and humidity, in the lightest and most ecological way possible.

Making an entrance

Arrival at the Eden Project is an experience in itself as the old quarry site is inconspicuous in the green Cornish countryside. Reaching its edge is like coming across a 'lost world'. The crater made by the old mine workings is almost 90 m (300 ft) deep, and so the biomes are only revealed as the visitor passes over the lip of the quarry en route to the Visitor Centre.

The Visitor Centre is the first contact with Eden and it underlines the idea that learning is a cornerstone of the project. It informs those arriving about what they are going to see so that they look at things with intelligent eyes. The Visitor Centre has a full array of audiovisual aids giving details of the plant population and the different climates to be encountered and is set neatly into the contours at the top of the site, giving sweeping views of the biomes below.

Visitors make their way down meandering paths to the turf-roofed connection point between the biomes. This structure, called the Link Building, with its café and restaurant, gives visitors a moment to reflect before they continue their exploration. With its glazed elevation it offers views of the landscaped pit, which represents a cool, temperate climate.

Moving to the smaller of the two biomes, visitors can observe the Mediterranean climate – of particular interest since global warming is apparently causing those areas of the world with this climate to enlarge dramatically. The other biome, arguably the most spectacular part of the whole Eden Project, showcases the humid tropics. Here the scale of the planting and the route that has been devised through it means visitors are barely aware of the enclosure and can immerse themselves in the extraordinary experience of a simulated rainforest. A further attraction is the waterfall down the cliff face. The sound of the water falling greatly adds to the atmosphere.

Looking to the future
As I write, plans for a third biome are taking shape. This will encapsulate the climate and vegetation of a desert region. Once again we are pushing the potential of our chosen materials to extremes. We intend to use a vast elliptical cable net structure that will be 120 m (393 ft) wide in its largest dimension. This will support the same type of inflated ETFE pillows as we used before but because of the cables the effect will be lighter – almost an artificial sky. We continue to challenge ourselves as Eden persists in captivating the office.

The potential range of sensory perception that the architecture of this project engenders enthrals me. It has also made me deeply conscious to the fact that the survival of the green areas of our planet is a matter of fundamental importance to everyone. If our project in this lost valley in Cornwall attracts visitors from all over the world, and if they can learn something about the dynamic and changing world of architecture as they learn about the mysteries of the botanical world, then I believe we will have achieved something of which we can all feel proud.

this
other
eden

HUGH PEARMAN

Some people used to ask why the Eden Project continued to be so named, long after it was completed and opened. Should it not become the Eden Centre? But that would be to suggest that it was a finite object, which was never the intention. There is no once-and-for-all version. Eden is organic: it grows and changes. If you regard it as science fiction turned fact, in the service of nature, then 2001 was a singularly appropriate time for its opening, being the year of Kubrick's *Space Odyssey*. Like that film, it is an open-ended proposition.

With a significant expansion of Eden being planned as I write – one that more than doubles the original capital value of what quickly turned out to be only the first phase – this intriguing uncertainty adds to Eden's air of Camelot-like mystery. What will it eventually become, and where, exactly? When, in the summer of 2002, the BBC asked architecture commentators to nominate modern 'wonders of the world', the one most frequently put forward was Eden. The only surprise in this, perhaps, is that this was exactly the intention of Eden's founders, and so it proved. A wonder was what they demanded, and a wonder was what they got. Even so, public acceptance of what constitutes a wonder is a notoriously fickle thing. Other millennial projects foundered: some, most notably the Millennium Dome, became objects of sustained media ridicule for political rather than architectural reasons. Eden, however, retained its aura. Why is this?

The other key movie reference is more arcane: the 1971 sci-fi cult classic *Silent Running*. There, the big idea was of spaceships that could be botanical

removed from the conventional practice of architecture would be hard to imagine. In that sense it was the ideal project for people whose take on architecture is always questioning.

The influences behind Eden

Seeing Eden at six distinct phases of its existence has made me realize how quickly we absorb and normalize the extraordinary. Those phases were: the early concept stages; the eventually approved design; the place as it was being built; then as it was just before opening; how it looked in 2002 after a year of high-intensity use; and how it may look by 2007 and after, given the present expansion plans. You have to remind yourself that this particular Eden was, at the time the project was conceived in the mid-1990s, just the Bodelva clay pit. Never visited or even known about by the public, it was a nearly exhausted lode of china clay in a region of mid-Cornwall – known as the 'clay country' – pockmarked with such active or abandoned mineral workings. The spoil tips rising into the sky mirror the pits sinking into the earth. With the industry still active but in decline, this was a high unemployment area, centred on St Austell, helped to some extent by the summer tourist trade of the West Country. Until Eden, ideas for regenerating the area had tended to be confined to small industrial units, though Smit's horticultural restoration project at nearby Megavissey, adroitly marketed as 'The Lost Gardens of Heligan', showed that people will travel great distances to see what he would call a Big Fat Idea.

So from then – moonscape of a quarry in an industrially scarred area – to now – a place acknowledged as a wonder – is a giant leap. However, people adjust to this. After all, it is there. Because it is there, obviously it could be done. We become blasé. So Eden has to develop, not only in order to continue to surprise, but in order to fulfil its original remit as an ideas generator as much as a building. It has to become a place which cannot be experienced all in one go, and which does more things for more people. In the meantime, getting from concept into physical reality has, among much else, advanced the art and science of architecture and engineering.

Eden is part of architecture's unending search for transparency and lightness: a quest that can be traced back to the rise of medieval Gothic cathedrals, which exploited the strength of the pointed arch as a means to dissolve the walls, so allowing large areas of glazing made up of innumerable tiny pieces of coloured and clear glass. The contrast with the massive masonry of the earlier round-arched Romanesque churches and cathedrals is remarkable: that was an architectural step-change if ever there was one. What with that and the incredibly tight tolerances achieved by the master stonemasons – nothing rough and ready about those buildings – it is in that period that you find the roots of what later came to be termed high-tech. The quest continued through Tudor times in England with the 'prodigy houses' of the Elizabethan architect Robert Smythson – Wollaton, Longleat and Hardwick Hall – with their unprecedented deployment of huge areas of glass, again achieved with small individual pieces. Later came the enormous advances of the Industrial

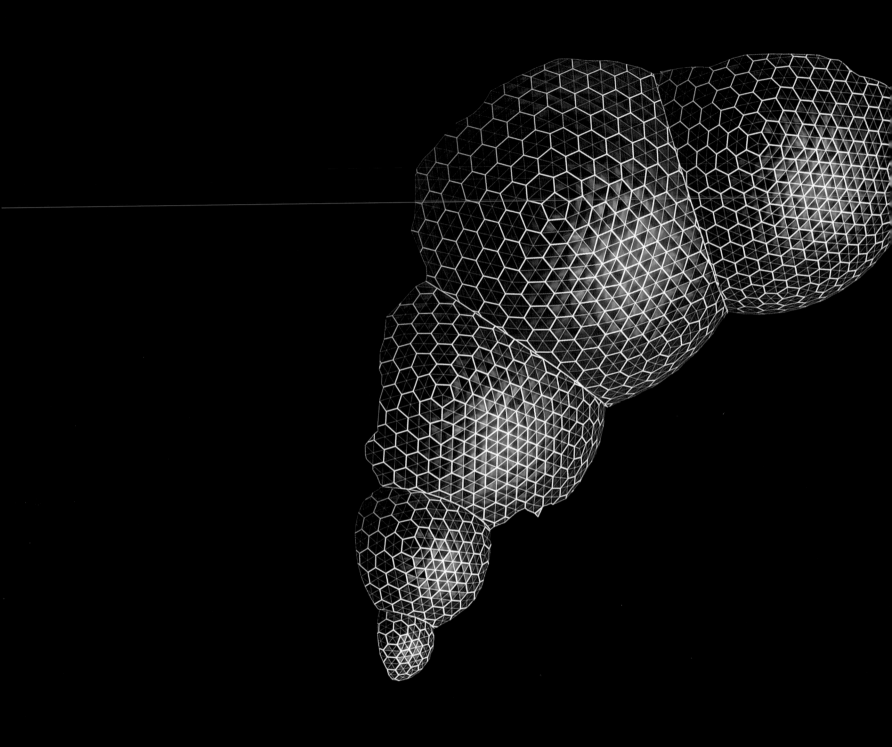

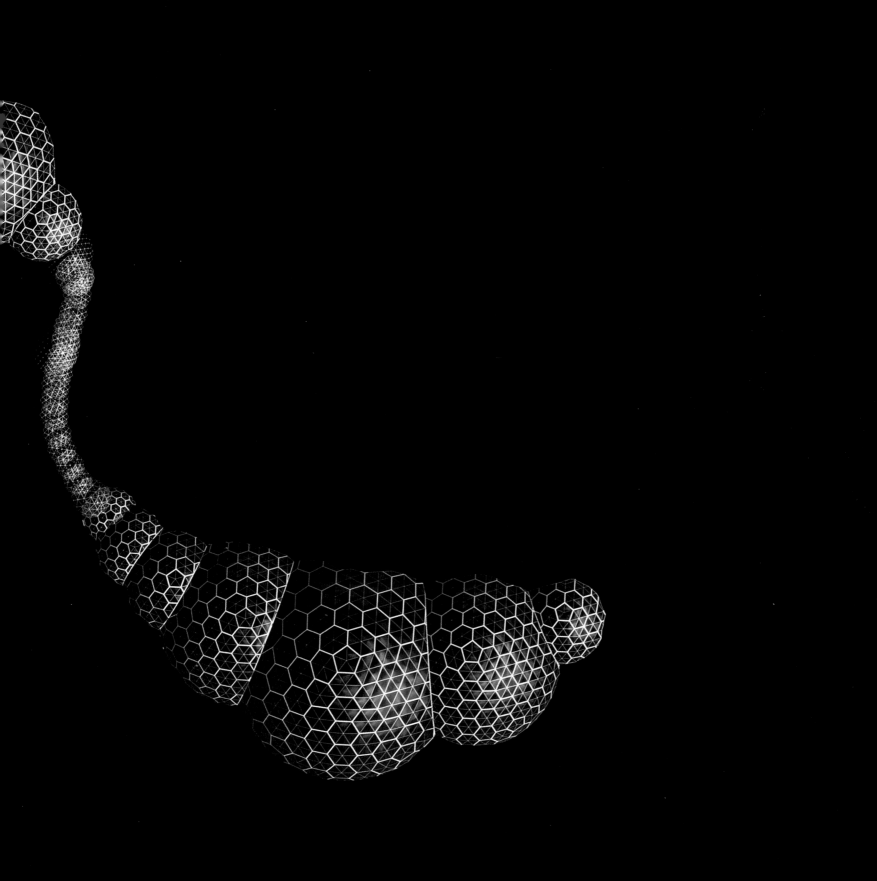

TOP LEFT AND RIGHT, BOTTOM LEFT
Early models built to explore
the Waterloo-inspired
structural solution of the
first scheme.

BOTTOM RIGHT
Computer model of the
first design for an inflated
ETFE glazing 'pillow'.

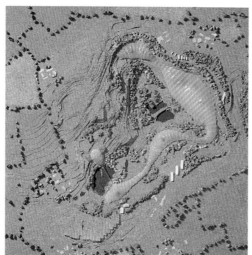

Revolution, which allowed steadily larger sheets of glass, and ever more slender framing components, in particular those made from wrought iron. Andrew Whalley, director in charge of architecture for the Eden Project, takes up the history of the botanical glasshouse in his essay later in this book.

This is significant because it was Grimshaw expertise in one particular large-span glazed enclosure that led to the practice being approached by Smit and his architect-adviser, Jonathan Ball, in 1995. Ball, with commendable selflessness, recommended that a project of such ambition required architects of international calibre and expertise. According to Smit, it came down to a choice between Grimshaw and Renzo Piano of Italy because both had recently completed highly advanced glazed transport interchanges: Kansai Airport in Japan by Piano, and Waterloo International Terminal in London by Grimshaw. Apparently the Englishness of Grimshaw counted in its favour: perhaps more to the point, the organic, asymmetrically curving precedent set by Waterloo (the first London terminus for international Eurostar trains) seemed to suggest a response to the contours of the Bodelva pit.

Eden: first thoughts
Although there had been preliminary studies for Eden carried out by Ball for Smit, at first working on the basis of a level site, by the time Grimshaw was brought in the search was concentrating on the clay pits of the area. There were plenty to choose from, but they were by no means all ideal. Many were still surrounded by dusty and all-too-visible industry. The idea of great

botanical glasshouses covered in a fine dust did not appeal. But then – a late entrant in the site search – the Bodelva pit came up. Still in use, it was, however, earmarked for closure as its clay ran out. Being set on top of a hill, it was like a crater; and being surrounded by dense woodland, it was like a lost world. There was a moment when Nicholas Grimshaw and the team pushed their way through the undergrowth to the lip of the crater and looked down at the giant trucks crawling around so far below that they looked like toys. Had the trucks been dinosaurs, it would not have seemed surprising. A shimmering blue lake filled part of the bottom of the pit. Vegetation and water cascaded down. Through a nick in the skyline to the south, you could see the sea. That first day, the essentials of Eden were born. The shape and aspect of the Bodelva pit generated the form of the building.

The idea was to use the cliff, to lean the glasshouses up against a wall of greenery, to wrap around the contours of the pit, and essentially to face southwest. Eden was to be the biggest lean-to greenhouse in the world. This seems thoroughly logical now, but at the time it was by no means the only option. Placing the glasshouses in the centre of the bottom of the pit, for instance, would have been an easier solution. But beyond the desire to face southwest, two things drove the practice's instinctive response. One was that by setting the enclosed biomes against the cliffs, more room was made for the open-air Cool Temperate Biome outside, a sheltered space that would exploit Cornwall's famously mild, Gulf Stream-warmed, climate. The other was an aesthetic response. In a greenhouse built on the flat – such as the famous examples at Kew Gardens in London – you can see out on all sides. You know you are in a man-made container. But with the lean-to arrangement, with a wall of vegetation rising up and curving round on one side, you are immersed in the environment. Once inside, it is possible to forget the container, which becomes a recessive rather than an intrusive presence.

The first Grimshaw concept for Eden – essentially a sketch model to explore the siting and the scale and nature of the spaces envisaged – involved exactly the same team as had worked on Waterloo, including the noted structural engineer and long-time friend of the practice, Anthony Hunt. This Mark 1 model derived its form from Waterloo. Long curving arches of varying sizes set against the sides of the pit allowed a curving and undulating glazed roofline, swelling into three enclosed 'biomes' or climate zones – tropical, temperate and desert. A large interpretation centre, at first taking the form of a giant leaf, descended into the pit to face the sinuous run of glasshouses. Although this structural solution and the design of the interpretation centre were later to change totally, the key moves had all been made. The scheme was costed at £106m. It was submitted to the Millennium Commission. It was rejected outright.

This was to be the first of several occasions when the mettle of the team was severely tested. The client, Tim Smit, was undaunted. He took the decision to continue as if nothing had happened. The design was refined, re-presented and again rejected. At which point, many people would have given up. The word going about at the time in London was that Eden was 'wobbly', that it would never get its finance together,

that the Millennium Commission was getting increasingly nervous of over-ambitious schemes going belly-up because they could not possibly generate the visitor numbers that their business plans suggested. It was at this point that a total redesign of the buildings took place, while maintaining all the key ingredients of the first, instinctive, response. As sometimes happens in such circumstances, this test of fire provoked an inspired response. Eden went lightweight.

The defining of Eden

Both Nick Grimshaw and Tony Hunt were lifelong admirers of the American engineer, designer and 'Spaceship Earth' philosopher Richard Buckminster Fuller (1895–1983). Fuller had, in the 1940s, developed the geodesic dome in a search for the most minimal form of large enclosure possible. His United States Pavilion at Expo '67 in Montreal (the year Nicholas Grimshaw first started in architectural practice) was his largest-scale realization of the geodesic principle, which he had envisaged being extended as an enclosure for entire cities. As with all great architectural thinkers, his ideas ran ahead of the available technology. The US Pavilion, clad in transparent acrylic panels, was devastated by fire although the skeleton remains. But by the late 1990s, developments both in materials and in computer-aided design and manufacturing techniques prompted Grimshaw and Hunt to return to Fuller. This was to be the salvation of the Eden Project.

One of Fuller's favourite questions was 'How much does the building weigh?' The answer, in the case of the redesigned Eden, is 'no more than the air inside it'.

TOP LEFT
Working model built
to investigate geodesic
principles for the final
scheme.

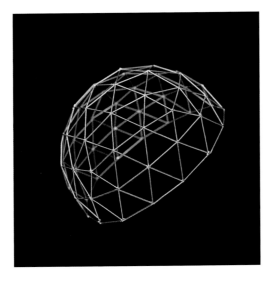

TOP RIGHT
Final model showing the
finished scheme and
planting in context.

BOTTOM
Computer rendering
created to demonstrate
the intersection of the biome
spheres and the ground
plane, shown as a red line.

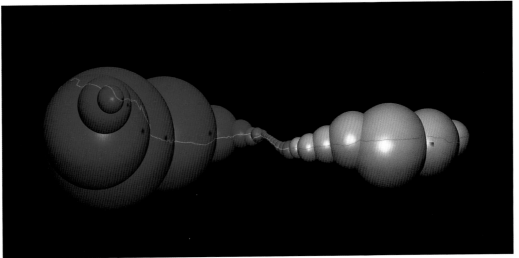

View of Bodelva before construction.

By modifying Fuller's geodesic concept to a series of intersecting domes made up principally of lightweight hexagonal steel components, and by choosing inflated triple-layer 'pillows' of ETFE translucent foil rather than glass, which is heavy and can perform unpredictably, the enclosed biomes of Eden transmuted into something less like a conventional glasshouse, more like a series of soap bubbles. The fact that this kind of structure is frequently encountered in nature, from honeycombs to the compound eyes of insects, both suggested that its designers were working along the right lines structurally, and chimed in with the aims of Eden. The buildings had acquired a layer of metaphor.

More pragmatically, the soap-bubble approach suited the changing contours of the site. With clay extraction still going on – the site survey had revealed pockets of clay that the pit's owners then proceeded to extract with high-pressure water jets – Grimshaw and Hunt were in the curious and frustrating position of trying to design buildings for a site that constantly altered its shape. Heavy rains, which tended to provoke landslips, did not help. Moreover, the original steel-arch solution would have meant some severe reshaping of the given landscape in order to make it fit. The geodesic solution, in contrast, could just settle lightly on the landscape, whatever its shape, in just the way that soap bubbles can. It could adapt very readily.

There is another advantage to the bubble solution. Where bubbles on the ground intersect, it is a law of nature that the point of intersection is vertical. That is just the way things are. To achieve this, the intersecting bubbles of Eden had to be calculated as pure sections of spheres. You could imagine them as being merely the tops of vast underground globes, some magical subterranean city or life form exposed by the processes of mining and erosion. Each of the two biomes – Humid Tropics and Warm Temperate – is conceived as the top of four such intersecting globes, which if they really existed in their entirety, would plunge hundreds of feet into the earth. This kind of highly mathematical setting out of a building is by no means new – Sir Edwin Lutyens was a master at it, and his 1920 national war memorial, known as the Cenotaph, in London's Whitehall, derives much of its subtle power from being conceived as a fragment of a greater, and invisible, whole. It is at such moments that architecture can sometimes appear to be something of a mystic art. In fact, it is simply painstaking geometry, the calculations for which are these days made infinitely easier by computing power.

Unlike conjoined soap bubbles – the skins of which form walls at the point of intersection – a building made in this way can do away with such walls. Instead, the point of intersection becomes a true arch, made inevitable by the spherical geometry. Similarly, the purity of the setting-out process means that the intersecting domes – effectively the sliced-off tops of the imaginary below-ground spheres – can adapt happily to changing ground conditions. They can ride over humps, descend into dips, simply by adding or subtracting some of the components that go to make up the structure.

Section drawn to demonstrate mature plant life in the Humid Tropics Biome.

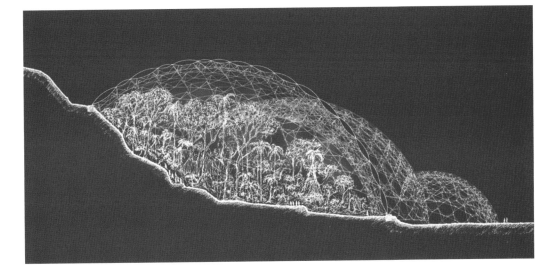

First things first: the Visitor Centre

If the enclosed biomes are what immediately grab the attention at Eden, from the moment the top of the Humid Tropics Biome rises from the earth as you approach it, a complementary role is played by the Visitor Centre. After initial ideas for a large multimedia building were abandoned as part of the cost-cutting exercise, a completely different approach was adopted over one busy weekend. What emerged from this pencil-and-notebook process was a scimitar-shaped building perched on the hillside looking across the crater to the biomes. This is the point of arrival. It takes the form of a street covered with a tensile fabric canopy. Tucked into the hillside to one side are lavatories and offices. On the curving side overlooking the pit are the restaurant and shop.

The scimitar building takes the form of a single, long, column-free space beneath an uptilted roof. With glazing and cedar-shingle cladding on its outer edge, its most visible feature from the arrival 'street' is its pinkish, rammed-earth rear wall. This ancient building technology, using earth from the pit, requiring no firing, and thus containing very little embodied energy, immediately serves to establish Eden's credentials. Being used as a free-standing infill wall for a steel-framed building in this way is not so very different from the medieval use of rammed earth or 'daub' as infill panels in prefabricated timber buildings. However, the effect in this context is wholly modern.

In any other setting, the Visitor Centre would attract considerable attention as a building in its own right. Indeed, during the year 2000 when nearly half a million visitors came to watch Eden being built, this was the only completed building, acting as a taster for the main act to follow and working, as intended, as an exhibition gallery and look-out point across the crater. But the fate – and consequent success – of this building is to be largely ignored, to fade into the background, to be subservient to the great domes across the way. It was originally laid out as a café, shop, plant sales and exhibition gallery, with dividing walls between the sections. Following the first year of operation, when nearly two million visitors came rather than the 750,000 conservatively predicted, these walls were removed and the space opened up, to great effect functionally and visually.

By way of comparison, in its first year of operation – despite the restrictions on movement in the British countryside caused by a severe nationwide outbreak of the cattle disease known as foot-and-mouth – Eden attracted considerably greater numbers than the celebrated Guggenheim Museum in Bilbao in its equivalent first year. This is significant. Towns and cities around the world now try to replicate the 'Guggenheim effect', having previously regarded with equivalent envy the economic and cultural impact of, for instance, the Sydney Opera House. At Eden, this profile-raising regenerative effect was achieved in open country, far from large cities (Plymouth and Exeter being the nearest) and with relatively poor public transport links. Given this, it was perhaps not surprising that the Millennium Commission at first regarded the project as over-ambitious. For all the success of Smit's Lost Gardens of Heligan, and of the Tate Gallery's outpost at St Ives – both of which had proved the hunger for cultural attractions in the

24

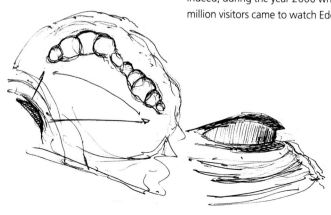

Andrew Whalley sketch explaining the relationship between the Visitor Centre and the biomes.

Views of the biomes
under construction.

southwest – this seemed like one hell of a shot in the dark. But in the end, it was the scale of Eden's ambition that brought the visitors flocking, and it is to the credit of the client and the Millennium Commission that the refined scheme was pursued and financed.

Eden under construction

When the china clay workers finally departed, the preparation work at Bodelva was mainly to do with stabilizing the site: in particular draining it, and restraining crumbling areas of cliff. This civil-engineering exercise was thoroughly daunting, not least because of the torrential rains that lashed Cornwall as work got under way. At one point, the section of the side of the pit destined to receive the Visitor Centre simply collapsed in a muddy mess, while the whole pit tried to turn itself into an enormous lake. The work of engineers and contractors in preparing the site under these extreme conditions cannot be over-emphasized. Apart from anything else, the drainage of Eden is, in consequence, a marvel. But in the meantime, the architecture had developed its own momentum.

The freedom provided by the geodesic principle allowed standard components to be made, most notably the galvanized tubular steel hexagons and part-hexagons of the domes (in many variants to cope with the irregular ground condition and various openings, but boiling down to four main sizes, proportional to the sizes of the larger and smaller domes). Beneath the hexagons is a lightweight triangulated space-frame support structure, acting in composite in what is called a hex-tri-hex system and which replicates the structure of a particular carbon molecule. The castings that form the node points of this structure are objects of great beauty in themselves, even if – being subsumed into the greater order of things – they are scarcely noticed by the visiting public. Finally, fixings were placed on top of the hexagons to hold securely the edges of the triple-layer pillows of inflated ETFE foil that would glaze them.

This was by far the largest such application of ETFE in the world. As the domes were constructed, rising from their undulating concrete strip foundations, they were also supported by the largest single assemblage of conventional scaffolding in the world, which itself took four months to build. This was the contractor's choice of construction methodology, and in its traditional way seemed somewhat at odds with the

Individually numbered biome node components.

progressive, clip-together image of Eden, but it worked very well. In fact, it was essential because, somewhat like the arch of a bridge, a geodesic dome only attains its strength when the final piece is in place. Until that moment, it has to be supported. The forest of scaffolding poles and planks certainly weighed considerably more than the delicate latticework of hexagons being constructed above them, but of course all that temporary material would subsequently be used elsewhere, so the principles of Eden remained uncompromised.

Less happy from the sustainability point of view is the currently inescapable international nature of large construction works of this kind. Although the Eden structure is made of British steel, for instance, that steel had to travel to four other countries during its fabrication into the final components of the biomes, eventually arriving by sea at the little port of Par before making the final short journey to site via flatbed truck. The embodied energy of the components is therefore quite high, in contrast to such purely local elements such as the rammed-earth wall of the Visitor Centre, or the stone walling of the approach roads. But set against this are the facts that Eden is as lightweight a building as today's technology allows for its given strength, that the small energy consumption needed to keep the foil pillows inflated is vastly compensated for by their superb insulating properties, that natural ventilation through the biomes is highly efficient, and that the structures are designed, so far as possible, to be 'future proof'. The ETFE foil will have a life of maybe 40 years; longer than heavy conventional glass installations last without major overhaul. At which

point, more advanced 'breathing' foils will be available, possibly with a degree of built-in reactive sun-shading. The skin (which is recyclable) can then very simply be replaced with the more advanced version, so vastly increasing the lifespan of the structures.

The making of the domes proceeded rapidly, subject to occasional setbacks such as floods, which at one point inundated the entire site. A moment of epiphany occurred when the first of the hexagons (apart from a test module made by the manufacturers Mero in Germany) was glazed with its pillow of ETFE. As the glazing continued, the character of the domes changed utterly, visually becoming living organisms rather than skeletons. Rapidly, the iridescent bubbles spread over the structure. The design is such that most of the visible structure is on the inside. Consequently,

View of the completed biomes, 'like a series of soap bubbles'.

only very slender bolted joints, like strips of Meccano, separate the pillows externally, with short connector rods projecting at each intersection of the hexagons. What you see from the outside, then, is not structure but skin. A chameleon-like skin, constantly changing in appearance according to light conditions, supported effortlessly by, seemingly, not very much at all.

Joining the two covered biomes is a linking, turf-covered, 'saddle' building which forms the entrance and contains a spacious restaurant opening up to the gardens outside, as well as invisibly providing the service entrance to the complex from the rear. Like the Visitor Centre, this entrance – the Link Building – is a sizeable and interesting steel-framed construction in its own right, arranged internally on two levels so that traffic between the two enclosed biomes does not disturb the sitting-around areas below. In the overall composition of Eden, it acts as a focus to the natural amphitheatre of the site. Despite all this, its visual role is to play second fiddle to the drama of the biomes to either side, like a col between mountains.

Moving on

So one of the most original constructions of modern times came to be 'completed' early in 2001, by which time it had already acquired celebrity status. The main problem after that was coping with the floods of visitors, and this put pressure on all the facilities. At peak times the numbers of people moving through the biomes became so dense that Eden had to close for short periods, and the surrounding roads became choked. Characteristically of the client, this

problem immediately became an opportunity. There had originally been a plan for a third biome dealing with desert conditions: if this could now be built, it would help to absorb all the visitors and spread them around the site more evenly. Temporary structures, which had sprung up during the first year of operation – not least for the enormous numbers of schoolchildren visiting – could be gathered into permanent buildings. Visiting academics could have their own research centre. Since the success of the project had highlighted the dearth of good visitor facilities in the area, a hotel and conference centre could become part of the mix.

Thus, during the first year of operation, Grimshaw architects returned to Eden with their sketchbooks – this time not to redesign in order to cut costs, but to build on its success. This new phase, being more diffuse than the original and including a number of separate, smaller buildings, many of them outside the original Bodelva pit, will in no way dilute the impact of the original built scheme. What it does do is revisit the original blue-sky idea and put back into the mix all the elements that were regretfully omitted along the way.

The first of these is the Eden Foundation, completed at the end of 2002 and designed to provide a comfortable working environment for Eden staff. The building is simply a timber box wrapped inside a lightweight metal skin and is both naturally ventilated and lit. It is the most sustainable building the practice has ever completed, in line with the Eden Project philosophy.

At the time of writing, other proposals in development include an Education Centre, a Visitor

Computer-generated sequence to analyze the final structural forms of the biomes and their location on the site.

28

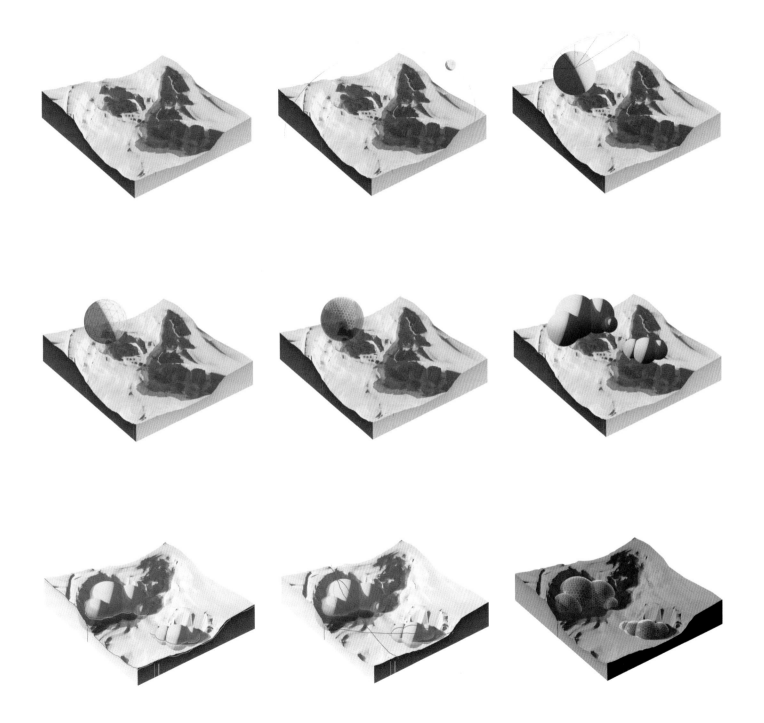

Gateway building, further staff facilities and the long-planned Dry Tropics Biome. This 'desert' biome reinterprets the hex-tri-hex structural system. It uses a similarly lightweight structure clad in ETFE foil but rather than following geodesic principles it adopts a distorted 'cable-net' form, with a perimeter structural ring. This solution, required because of the necessity for brighter light than in the other biomes, is possible because the soft fill site earmarked does not require a structure adaptable to changes in the ground profile, unlike those of the previous biomes.

The evolution of the glasshouse thus continues. Just as the first structural idea for the biomes was replaced with the geodesic solution better adapted to the conditions, so the projected third biome, on level ground, can take a different approach again. The family of structures at Eden is developing, each a reasoned response to changing circumstances rather than being an imposed aesthetic solution.

Such elements were under intense discussion as this book went to press. As with the original phase of Eden, there are countless changes along the way as hard reality shakes hands with idealism. Perhaps the greatest achievement of Eden – which is nothing to do with the architecture, and everything to do with the people behind the project – is to blur the distinction between the two, such that everyone becomes involved and committed. But as part of that alchemical process, an old architectural dream is being realized. Yes, it can be done. High architecture can provide immense popular appeal across all social groupings – so long as the content of the buildings, the underlying idea, is in itself strong and necessary. It thus becomes what architectural idealists have always imagined: a means to an end, a continuing process, rather than an end in itself.

LEFT
View of a partially glazed biome in evening sunlight.

BELOW
Cutaway perspective drawing of the third, Dry Tropics, biome.

the
architecture
of
eden

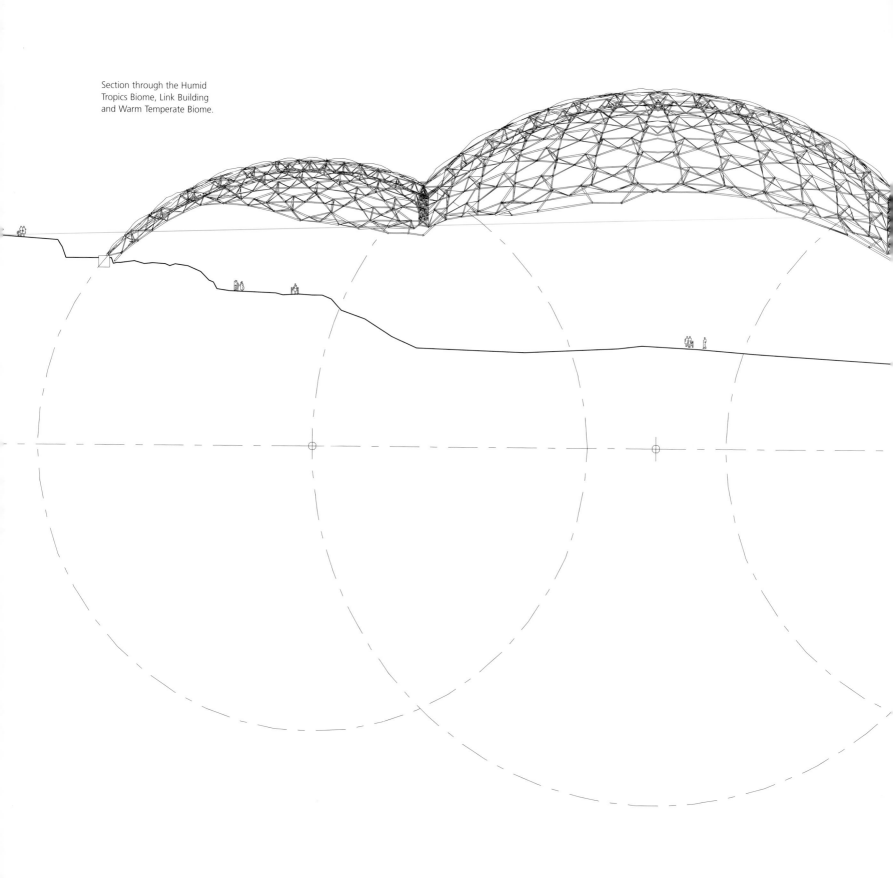

Section through the Humid
Tropics Biome, Link Building
and Warm Temperate Biome.

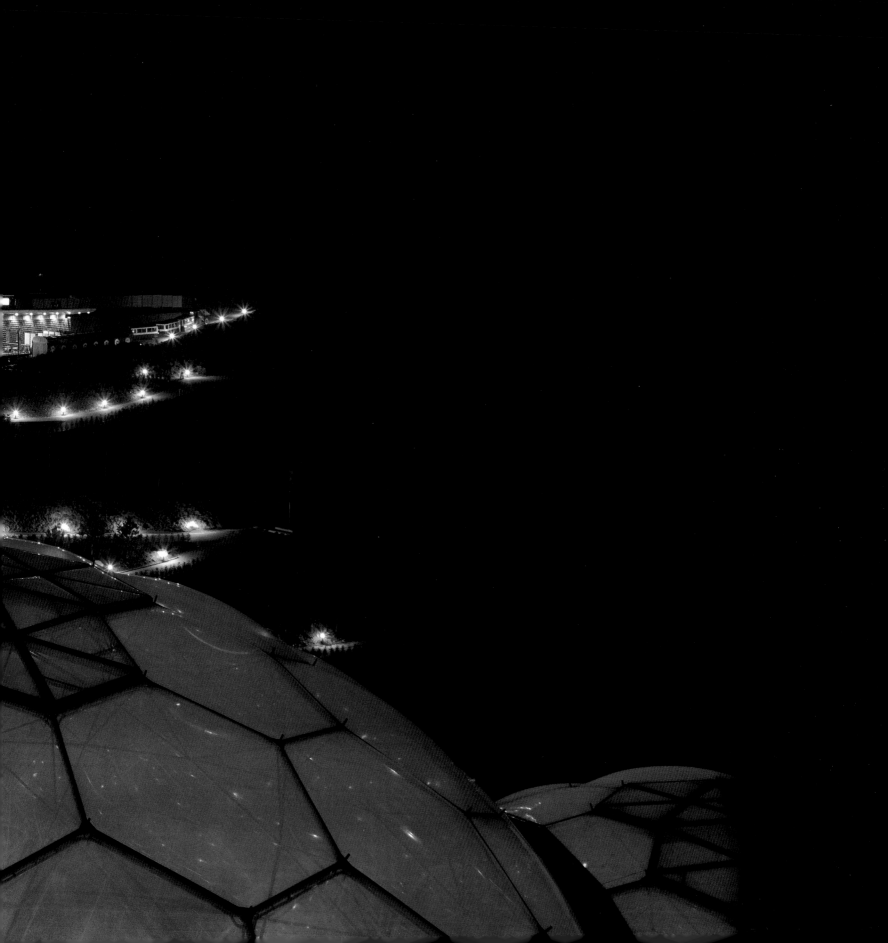

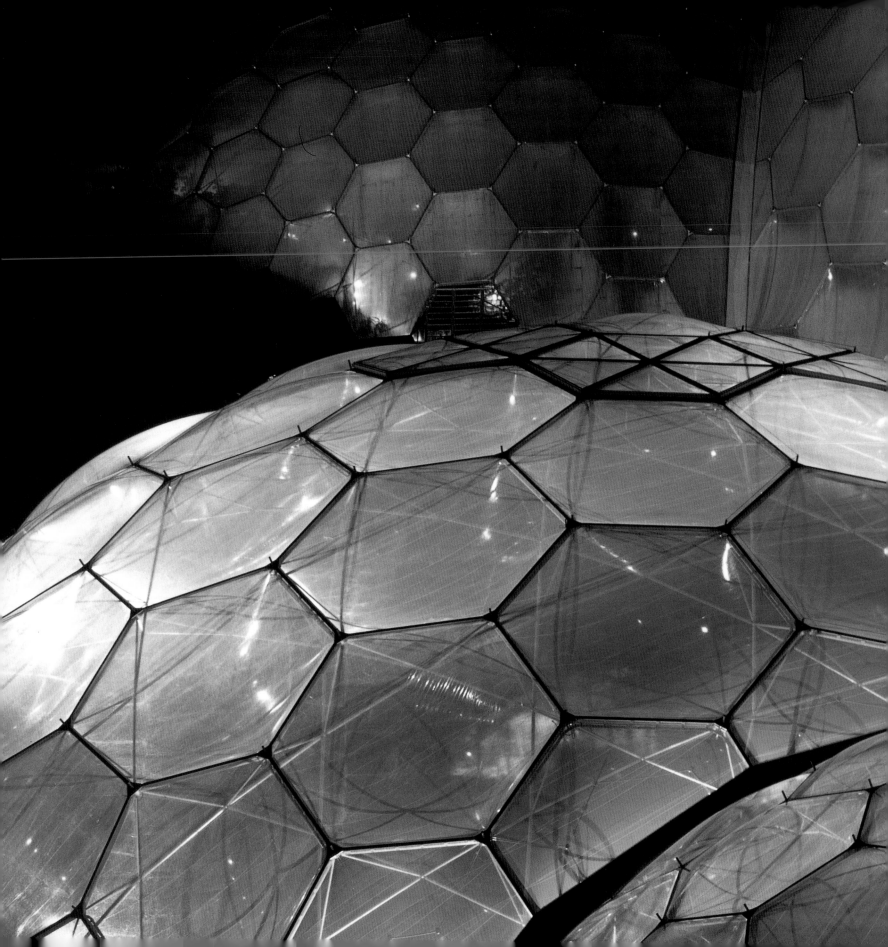

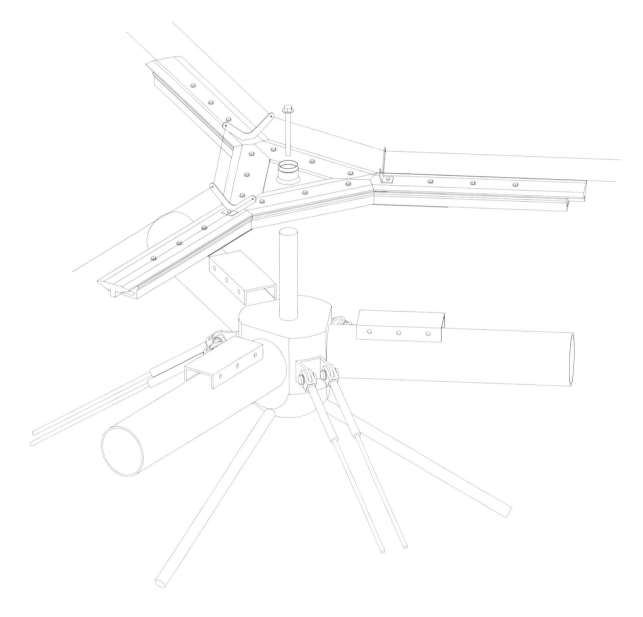

Exploded axonometric drawing
of the biome node detail.

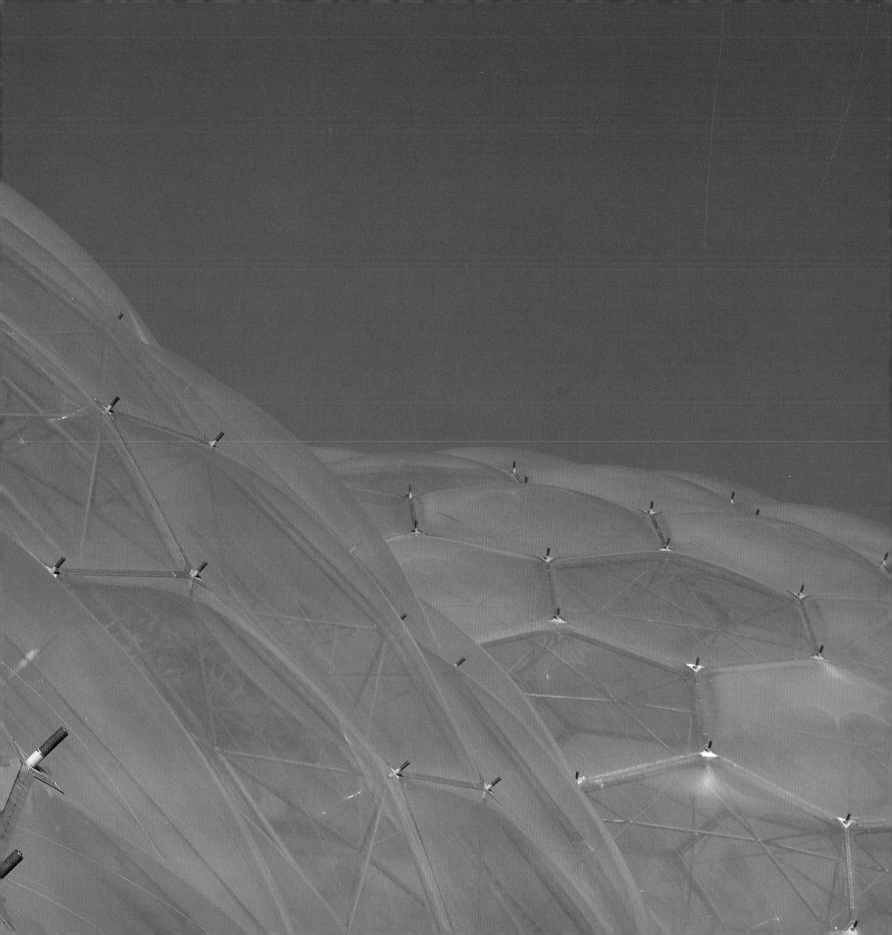

eden
visitor
centre

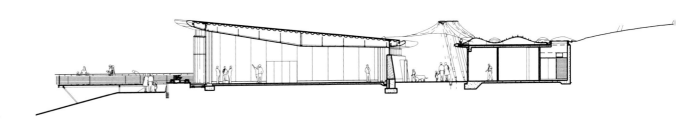

eden
foundation

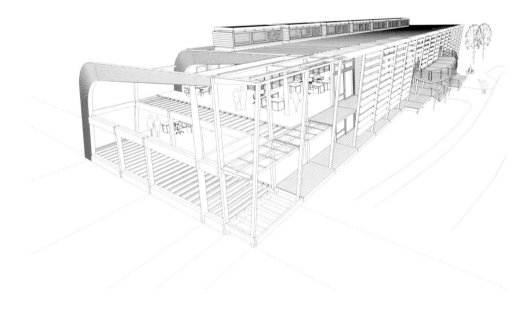

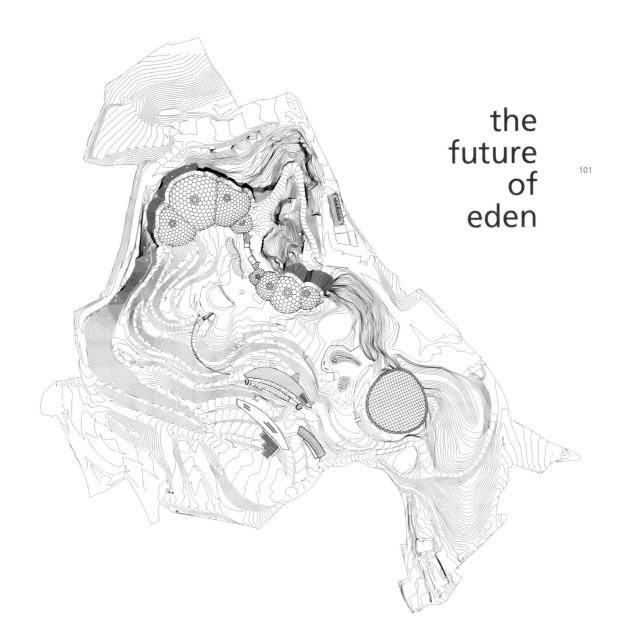

the
future
of
eden

PREVIOUS PAGE
The masterplan showing
all four phases of the project,
from the Visitor Centre
to the Dry Tropics Biome.

102

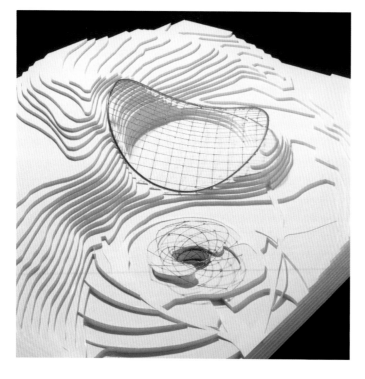

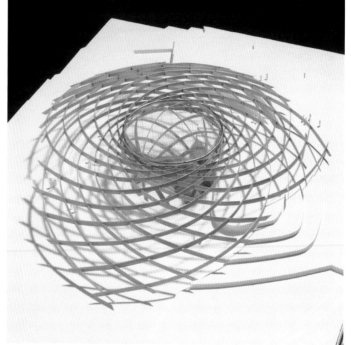

ABOVE
Sketch model showing the
new biome and the
Education Centre.

ABOVE RIGHT
Detail model of the proposed
'double Fibonacci spiral'
structure for the Education
Centre, based on the
geometry of a pine cone.

RIGHT
Computer rendering of the
planned Dry Tropics Biome
with its 'anticlastic' cable-net
structure, which at any given
point is in double curvature.

eden
and the
glasshouse
tradition

ANDREW WHALLEY

Glasshouse design continues to inspire pioneering architects and engineers. The monumental Palm House at Kew, the curving splendour of Kibble Palace in Glasgow, Richard Buckminster Fuller's cities encased in glass domes, the flowing form of Foster's Great Glass House in Wales and, of course, the Eden Project, are major cornerstones in the evolution of glasshouse design. With their innovative structural solutions and use of materials, the pioneers have each played their part in influencing Grimshaw's work at Eden.

Without plants there would be no life on earth. Almost all our energy sources come from the sun; plants convert the sun's energy through photosynthesis and supply us with our vital support systems – oxygen, food, fuel, medicine and clothes. Glasshouses are essential to man's relationship with plants; they allow man to grow plants that would never survive in the open air of that particular region, and our civilization is inexorably entwined with developments in plant exploitation. The simultaneous blooming of plant science and the Industrial Revolution in the nineteenth century created a catalyst for a new type of architecture – the glasshouse.

The earliest glasshouses

The earliest written record of man manipulating the environment to grow plants comes from Plato's descriptions of the Gardens of Adonis in about 400 BC, when women ritually planted seeds in pots in honour of the God. Plato wrote: 'A grain of sand, or the branch of a tree placed in or introduced into these gardens, acquires in eight days a development which cannot be obtained in many months in the open.' Sadly, we can only guess at the hothouses of the ancient world, although there is evidence of glass making even in Egyptian times. We do know that the Romans split marble and onyx to make translucent sheets for plant propagation. But it was not until the Renaissance that gardens and buildings dedicated to exploring plant science appeared. The trade routes of Venice and Genoa introduced new plant species to Europe from the East in the mid-sixteenth century. Botanical gardens, complete with 'viradiums', or greenhouses, were set up from Pisa to Florence. These structures were of masonry rather than glass, fitted with braziers for heat and used to propagate and shelter plants.

During the seventeenth century, the search for new, and potentially lucrative, plant species intensified, particularly in the seafaring nations of Holland and Britain. Enthusiasm for nurturing these new specimens grew, and in 1654 Sir Hugh Platt published his thoughts on forcing and greenhouse design entitled *The Garden of Eden*. Despite this new fervour, the architectural response was still no more than a well-lit masonry building – the orangery. These provided shelter during the cold winter months, but for full propagation plants were moved outside for the summer. Undoubtedly a romantic building, the orangery was a testimony to the aristocratic love affair with plants and landscape. One of the most grandiose is Jules Hardouin-Mansart's south-facing example at Versailles, finished in 1686. Many would later be transformed into fully-fledged glasshouses, their slate roofs replaced with glass.

The Palm House,
Bicton Gardens, Devon

W. & D. Bailey, 1820

Making use of glass's natural properties

The next 100 years brought many developments. A great eighteenth-century innovator was George Clifford, Anglo-Dutch financier and director of the Dutch East India Company, which transported many exotic plants back to northern Europe. Clifford indulged his interest in zoology and horticulture with a private menagerie at his country estate in Hatrekampin, Holland. But it was not the tigers and apes or the dramatic landscapes that attracted the critics' attention, but his glass hothouses. Clifford created an exotic jungle in temperate Holland and his structures (referred to at the time as 'houses of Adonis') were packed with plants from the tropics. These were the first true glasshouses; they used the greenhouse effect, where the infrared component of

solar radiation is allowed to enter the enclosure. As its wavelength changes it is captured and reflected back into the environment, creating a new artificial climate.

Clifford used an early control system, first developed in Holland. The glass walls let him alter the environment inside the hothouses. Timber panels provided insulation or were raised on pulleys as wind buffers, while canvas curtains protected the plants from the elements and layers of oiled paper formed a primitive double-glazing system. The system incorporated heated forcing frames – brick enclosures that formed planting 'sinks', warmed via a series of cavities and flues by hot air from coal fires.

It was not until the nineteenth century that this new horticultural science – understanding the importance of sunlight, orientation and environmental control – arrived in Britain. It was an exciting time. The growth of Empire lined Europe's pockets and brought with it an ever-increasing number of exotic and fragile plants. Yet there was no building where people could go to enjoy these rich tropical specimens. The Dutch forcing frames were strictly for growing plants, not for having parties. Orangeries, although enjoyed by their owners, did not offer the right environmental conditions for tropical specimens. A completely new architectural response was needed, spurred on by technical developments in industry and construction. The glasshouse was about to come into its own.

Materials were still fairly limited. Glass, an expensive luxury, was taxed according to the size of the panes. It was made either by spinning plates of molten glass (a time-consuming craft process) or by the cheaper method of slicing up cylinders of soft glass and rolling

them flat, into long but narrow rectilinear sheets. The obvious conclusion was to glaze these new plant houses with many small sheets rather than fewer large ones. Slender wrought-iron glazing bars, allowing for a more transparent skin, were more efficient than the traditional timber for holding the glass in place.

A new form of design

It was Thomas Knight, elected as head of the London Horticultural Society (LHS) in 1811, who provoked the next development in glasshouse design. He set out an irresistible challenge in his inaugural speech: 'Not a single building of this kind has yet been erected in which the greatest possible quantity of space has been obtained and of light and heat admitted – proportionate to the capital expended.' (Interestingly, this statement was repeated almost word for word by Peter Thoday, one of Eden's two horticultural directors, at the first briefing for the project.) Two Scotsmen who responded to Knight's speech would have a formidable influence on glasshouse design. They were Sir George Mackenzie and John Claudius Loudon.

Mackenzie proposed his new curved glasshouse design in a letter to the LHS in 1815. It would be parallel to the 'vaulted surface of the heavens' and would follow the movement of the sun through the atmosphere for maximum gain of heat and light. He would enhance this by using a glass and iron construction to optimize transparency. Mackenzie had just designed the first curvilinear glasshouse.

Meanwhile Loudon laid down the blueprint for principles that would govern a century of glasshouse projects. In 1816 he patented a technique exploiting

The Great Conservatory
('Great Stove'), Chatsworth

Joseph Paxton, 1836

the malleable qualities of wrought iron. He discovered that he could use it to make curved sash bars to hold glass panels, which offered possibilities for a new type of architecture and inspired his bell-shaped design for the LHS, made entirely out of glass and wrought iron. Its vertical sides would allow for more mature specimens to be grown and avoid the damage of dripping condensation. Ambitiously, it could be raised from its base using pulleys to allow full ventilation.

Loudon developed his ideas in his book *Remarks on Hothouses*. We should credit him with the invention of ridge and furrow glazing, where glass is manipulated into a series of inverted 'v' panels. He argued that a glass building with such a pleated envelope ensured that the sun's rays would be at right angles to the glass surface at sunset and sunrise and would 'catch the two daily meridians'. Loudon went on to develop this proposal into a complete environmental system. Condensation would be caught and drained through the iron glazing bars. Canvas blinds were to provide protection from the sun and provide insulation. Glass louvres could be pulled open by ropes for ventilation. These ropes would connect to James Kewley's patented design, the 'automaton gardener'. This ingenious automatic machine used weights and pulleys governed by mercury heat sensors, so that Loudon's ventilation panels would only open when the glasshouse became too hot.

While his thoughts on glasshouses made interesting reading, nothing is more persuasive than an actual building. So he went ahead and built an elaborate prototype at his home in London. He brought in manufacturers W. & D. Bailey to build the structure, which in time was to prove an even greater opportunity for them than for Loudon. Together they offered an early form of packaged design and build – Loudon and his associates marketing the ideas in Britain with W. & D. Bailey providing the construction package. Sadly, few of these early glasshouses survived. One exception, at Bicton in Devon, was possibly built after Loudon's death, but was a faithful execution of his ideas by W. & D. Bailey. Its elegant, filigree form is like the delicate structure of a leaf.

Loudon's ideas spearheaded what has become glasshouse design tradition – to use the latest and best technology to optimize the performance of the enclosure. His was an organic approach to design that dispensed with architectural preconceptions about applied style. Instead, the design was rooted in the building's function, the materials, and the technology used for its construction. Loudon explained: 'It may be beautiful without exhibiting any of the orders of Grecian or of Gothic design … may not therefore glass roofs be rendered expressive of ideas of a higher and more appropriate kind, than those which are suggested by mere sheds or a glazed arcade.' Loudon's vision would be developed and refined towards the end of the nineteenth century by two more familiar names (and often direct competitors): Sir Joseph Paxton and Richard Turner.

The work of Sir Joseph Paxton
Paxton is famous for the industrialization of the building process and most importantly his innovative

The Palm House,
Royal Botanic Gardens, Kew

Decimus Burton and
Richard Turner, 1845–8

approach to construction. His prefabrication techniques were to reduce construction time and cost dramatically. He remains one of the few household names in British construction history. After starting out as a labourer in the 1820s, Paxton went to work at the Chiswick National School for Propagation where he was promoted to assistant gardener and caught the eye of the Duke of Devonshire, who had ambitious plans for Chatsworth, his country estate. Here Paxton would be given the opportunity to demonstrate a talent for design and construction that would eventually see him knighted. As head gardener at Chatsworth, Paxton began to improve the existing glasshouses and build up the collection of plants. But he made his name with Chatsworth's great glass conservatory of 1841, known as the 'Great Stove'. The glass tax was repealed in 1840 and this would have almost certainly have encouraged such ambitious glazing. The architect Decimus Burton prepared the drawings; he was responsible for the proportions of the building, but the overall credit goes to Paxton, whose initial sketches of 1836 showed a large central arch that formed a long aisle resting on columns and stabilized by a smaller arch that followed the perimeter of the building.

Other than the cast-iron columns running the length of the aisle, the construction was wooden, with glue-laminated timber used for the central arch. When small strips of timber are glued together like this, their collective strength is far greater than a solid piece of wood of equivalent size would be. The Great Stove is famous for its ridge-and-furrow glazing, no doubt inspired by Loudon. The inverted 'v' form gave the glazing an east–west orientation and so minimized the loss of sunlight that is caused by the reflective nature of the glass.

The structure benefited from Paxton's newly developed mechanized building techniques, in particular the automated production of the timber sash bars (which held the glass). It is interesting to note that, despite being heralded as the great industrialist, he bypassed iron for more traditional timber glazing frames in all his glasshouses (including the Great Stove and the Great Exhibition building).

From Kew to Queen's Street Station
The Irish constructor and engineer Richard Turner is renowned for building the Palm House in the Royal Botanical Gardens at Kew in 1848, also in collaboration with Burton. While working at the Hammersmith Iron Works in Dublin, Turner cut his teeth on a series of glasshouse projects, notably the conservatory at the Belfast Botanical Gardens in 1839. He analysed the different qualities of cast iron, and concluded that for Kew, the more malleable wrought iron could be used for the arched structure and the glazing bars, reserving cast iron for the columns. Rather than using ridge-and-furrow glazing he preferred curved sheets of glass as they emphasized the curved structure and form. Turner used wrought-iron tie bars to post-tension the structure once it was all in place, creating a rigid but lightweight form – a technique that he then patented. His innovative approach produced a more delicate and transparent glasshouse than had ever been seen before. Unfortunately the Palm House was not entirely a success. The green-tinted glass used to prevent plant

scorching seemed to slow the plants' growth. Furthermore, downdraughts around the conservatory's edges prevented some of the perimeter from being used for delicate plants. But this was subsequently largely resolved by improvements to the heating system and also reglazing the conservatory with clear glass in 1895.

As with the Great Stove at Chatsworth, Burton's contribution was probably the overall proportions and conservatory profile, while Turner's was the technological input of a self-taught intuitive engineer. It is interesting to contrast the very lightweight form of the Palm House with the Temperate House at Kew, designed by Burton ten years later. Without the structural ingenuity of Turner, a pre-ordained architectural style took over. In contrast to the organic approach of the Palm House, Burton's Temperate House with its heavy stylized form looks as if it was the predecessor to Turner's design.

These exciting industrialized glasshouse designs were to influence the new railway architecture of the second half of the nineteenth century. The glue-laminated technique used for the arches of Chatsworth was taken up by Lewis Cubitt, and used for the first roofs at King's Cross Station in 1852. Immediately after finishing the Palm House, Turner went on to design iron and glass roofs over Roadstone Station in Dublin and Liverpool's Lime Street Station. Lime Street featured an efficient bowstring arch, which spanned 48 m (156 ft) and used the minimum number of components. Although it no longer exists, a similarly constructed roof can be seen today at Glasgow's Queen Street Station.

The Great Exhibition

The Lime Street roof was constructed in just ten months. So Turner would have been ideally placed when a Royal Commission, headed by Prince Albert, announced an international competition in 1850. The challenge was to design a great temporary hall in London to exhibit the 'Works of Industry of all Nations'. It had to be a large structure that could be rapidly assembled to open the following year. This was to be the famous Great Exhibition building of 1851.

This exhibition offered another opportunity to apply the ideas emerging in glasshouse and railway station design. The proposals for this exhibition hall, although not a glasshouse in the botanical sense, demonstrate the differing approaches of Turner and Paxton and are probably the best illustration of the potential of the new construction techniques.

Another great architectural tradition was heralded in 1850 – the badly run competition. The rules allowed the judges to name no overall winner, but to draw upon any of the ideas from the entries. Turner's proposal, one of 245 entries, was a wrought-iron tripartite arch structure supporting an overall shallow arch, enclosed with glass and timber. Though he received an honourable mention, Turner's design was thought to be unrealistic for the time available, probably because the designs included large amounts of wrought iron – a slow craft process compared to the more mechanized production of cast iron. The solution was literally 'design by committee', which cherry-picked Owen Jones and Charles Wild's idea for a large masonry building, and then topped

The Great Exhibition building,
London

Joseph Paxton, 1850–1

it with a great glass dome designed by Isambard Kingdom Brunel. The whole proposal was co-ordinated by the architect Sir Matthew Digby Wyatt. One can only imagine Turner's irritation, as this scheme could neither be built on time nor easily dismantled. It didn't even advocate dry construction, an idea put forward by many of the entrants, but reverted to traditional bricks and mortar. The feasibility of this proposal was questioned throughout the spring of 1850, and time was rapidly running out.

So Joseph Paxton, probably out of frustration and opportunism, took a chance. With breathtaking speed and bravado he organized a team and put forward his own proposals. There was only a year to go. He visited the site during the first week of June 1850 and on the 11th came up with his famous blotting paper sketch,

a simple diagram that captured the entire concept of his proposal. Paxton collaborated with the Midland Railways engineer William Henry Barlow (who would later design the large-span roof at London's St Pancras station). In just over a week a full set of scheme drawings were ready. In less than two weeks from his first sketch he had presented his drawn proposals to Prince Albert, and Lord Granville of the finance committee. He had also met Charles Fox of contractors Fox and Henderson and the Birmingham glass manufacturer Robert Chance. In just over two weeks more the team put in a joint bid to design, construct and dismantle the exhibition hall. Rather than simply offering a construction price (which in this case was £150,000) they suggested a lower price of £79,800 if the materials of the building remained their property. In other words, they could re-use and reconstruct it after the exhibition finished. This offer was extremely enterprising and attractive, and, perhaps more importantly, deliverable within the short deadline.

The final stumbling block was a row of mature elms in Hyde Park. There was a public outcry. So Paxton proposed a timber-arched roof to span over the trees. This was the only significant deviation from Paxton's first sketch a mere seven weeks earlier. His team signed a contract on 26 July 1850 to deliver a building covering 18 acres that would be ready to open to the public within ten months.

Under Paxton, the site of the Great Exhibition glasshouse quickly became a highly efficient building factory. His mechanized system churned out timber sash bars at the rate of nearly three miles a day. Even the painting was automated; the bars were whipped through a paint bath and then the excess paint brushed off. For the cast iron trusses (also made on site) Fox Henderson borrowed from the mass-production techniques initially used for railway buildings. They were to be weighed to check for air pockets and then pre-stressed using hydraulic jacks to provide uniformity in the truss depths over a variety of spans.

The key to Paxton's design was repetition and weight. Small and light components were easily lifted into place with block and tackle. The fast 'dry construction' was vital to the building's success. The frame could be raised quickly. The beams were placed into sockets in the columns, and then locked into place by hammering in two wedges. Even the hoarding

Kibble Palace,
Glasgow Botanic Gardens

John Kibble, 1873

around the site was re-used as open-board flooring, with gaps between the slats so the dust could be brushed away. The exhibition was an enormous success. Six million visitors marched through its doors during the building's six months on this site. Its legacy is the 'Albertopolis' area in London: buildings and institutions from the Albert Hall to the Victoria and Albert Museum were all funded by the Great Exhibition's proceeds. After the exhibition, Paxton's team simply packed up the hall and moved it to Sydenham where it survived for another eighty years as the Crystal Palace before its tragic destruction by fire.

Paxton's Great Exhibition was a major influence on Brunel for his 1854 iron-and-glass train shed at Paddington Station, also built by Fox Henderson.

Once again the techniques that had been developed for the glasshouse were transferred and developed for railway buildings, this time for its vast sheds.

From the industrialist to the craftsman

If Paxton was the great industrialist, then W. & D. Bailey and Richard Turner were the craftsmen of glasshouse design, using a fully integrated structural shell in more fluid, organic buildings. There can be no better example to illustrate this than the soft rolling forms of Kibble Palace. Engineer John Kibble built the glasshouse at the Kibble home in Coulport, Loch Long. But when it became clear that his wealthy Glaswegian merchant family had little interest in preserving the building, this enthusiast of engineering, botany, photography and astronomy donated it to the Glasgow Corporation. Kibble dismantled, shipped and reassembled the glasshouse in Glasgow's botanical gardens, covering the costs by charging an entry fee for special events and introducing large photographic projectors and sound and lighting effects to wow the public. A concealed orchestra played, filling the glass enclosure with music.

To step out of a cold wet Glasgow winter into a warm tropical world enhanced by Kibble's clever entertainments must have been a thrilling experience. I found this building enormously influential while I studied at the Mackintosh School of Architecture, and it was equally influential when we explored solutions for the Eden Project. As a young student I invited the engineer Tony Hunt to spend a few days at the architecture school and I also took him to see Kibble Palace, my favourite local building. Little did we

know then that we would be exploring similar themes together at Eden ten years later.

**New materials, new designs:
Buckminster Fuller**

The twentieth century was to introduce some groundbreaking developments in glasshouse construction and design, particularly when it came to experimenting with new materials such as acrylic plastics. Another advance was the fact that rolled steel could now be economically produced for hollow tubes or a variety of flat shapes and sections. Improved understanding of its properties, together with developments in mathematical ideas, opened up new possibilities for efficient lightweight glasshouses.

It is Richard Buckminster Fuller, inventor, designer and philosopher, who is inextricably linked to these mathematical ideas, notably geometrically subdividing a sphere. Fuller dedicated his life to the ideal of sustainable living, using natural and environmentally friendly resources. This inspired him to explore very efficient lightweight structures, constructing the stable form of the dome and sphere out of a series of short straight sticks. He analysed these 'geodesic' forms with his students and finally patented them as series of different geometric combinations.

Fuller's designs included a house based on a hexagonal plan, incorporating six triangular rooms, which could easily be taken down, transported and reconstructed. Along with empirical analysis of his structures were philosophical proposals for their application. One was to create completely new microclimates for individual homes or even for cities: his famous photomontage shows a dome enclosing a large part of Manhattan.

One of the first large-scale geodesic domes used as a glasshouse was the 1959 Climatron at the St Louis Botanical Gardens, USA. Aluminium tubes supported a triangular grid of acrylic sheets to make up this hexagonal-framed structure 54 m (177 ft) in diameter. It was not only ambitious architecturally, it also enclosed a range of climates in one building, from the humid heat of the tropics to the drier, more temperate Mediterranean. Doing this in one space proved a challenge, but was not as problematic as the enclosure itself. The acrylic sheets (which were always considered a short-term material) degraded in the harsh Mid-West environment and were replaced in 1988 with glass, necessitating a new inner dome capable of carrying the heavier material. The external dome now serves only as a decorative reminder of the earlier structure, which in some ways shows that the geodesic enclosure was an idea ahead of its time.

The sixties and seventies saw a whole series of adventurous enclosures constructed from strong, lightweight acrylic sheeting. In 1965 three domes were built in concrete and acrylic for the botanical gardens in Milwaukee, Wisconsin. Like Eden, each contained a different environment, from the humid tropics to the warm temperate, but avoided the technical difficulties of combining different 'climates' in a single space.

The exploration of plastic enclosures reached its zenith in 1967 with Fuller's dome for the Montreal Exposition. Developed in conjunction with architects the Cambridge Seven, the dome demonstrated the notion of a 'world within a world'. The original intention was that the skin would control the environment within, changing colour to give shade from the sun. Fuller adapted this idea, using six fabric roller blinds as shades for each hexagonal panel. As they were opened or closed a dynamic skin of changing pixelated panels was created, a concept that has intrigued and inspired architects ever since.

Glass versus more modern developments

Frustratingly, the advances in structural theory were way ahead of the material technology. The plasticizers in acrylic absorb ultraviolet light, causing brittleness and discoloration. But this was not the most worrying aspect of the material, as the tragic fire at the Summerland Complex on the Isle of Man was to prove in the 1970s. Acrylic sheeting is highly flammable and drips molten burning material as it disintegrates. The considerable loss of life at Summerland stopped its use in buildings.

As acrylic was abandoned, glass once more came to the forefront of structural exploration. But the late twentieth century saw the demise, in Britain at any rate, of the botanical glasshouse as a vehicle for artistic and engineering endeavour. Instead, British botanical gardens commissioned a series of disappointingly utilitarian glasshouses, owing more to the practicality of commercial market gardens than the inspirational forms of their predecessors.

The 1985 glass enclosures, or bioclimatic façades, for the National Museum of Science, Technology

United States Pavilion,
Expo '67 Montreal

Richard Buckminster Fuller, 1967

and Industry at La Villette in Paris are an exception, as their design resulted in exciting new construction developments. The architects and engineers Rice Francis Ritchie (RFR) wanted to create glass walls of optimum transparency to house bamboo plants. The tried and tested approach for a large wall like this was to hang glass sheets like a curtain, using glass fins as beams to strengthen the walls against the wind. But if one looked at these obliquely, one would see the many layers of glass fins rather than the clean line of the wall. So RFR hung the glass sheets, but instead supported them with thin, almost invisible, high-tensile cables in the form of opposing bowstring trusses. This system has now been developed and used throughout architecture.

A new material discovered in the 1950s, polycarbonate, brought a much-needed lease of life to developments in synthetic glasshouses. Frei Otto and Günter Behnisch created the Olympic Stadium for the 1972 Games in Munich by stringing high-tensile cables (as RFR had) into a net and then pulling them, under enormous force, so that they formed striking three-dimensional tent-like structures. The net was then covered with sheets of polycarbonate joined together by neoprene gaskets. These 'zipper gaskets' quite simply zip the sheets together. The construction ideas owed almost more to spiders' webs in nature than traditional building techniques. Spiders use net structures to cover very large areas with the minimum of material. At Grimshaw we are exploring this system in the design for the Dry Tropics Biome.

I have tried to explain how glasshouse design has exploited the potential of new materials in order to generate new architectural forms. But the latest developments are not about using a particular material; rather they focus on exploring new three-dimensional forms. Computer Aided Design has given us new opportunities to design buildings with more complex forms. We are no longer restricted by orthogonal, geometric design techniques. The second development is Computer Aided Manufacture. Short runs of sophisticated components and complex shapes are possible where before we relied on repetitive linear manufacturing systems to produce components cost-effectively. We can now design in a truly organic and free way, following the guiding principles of nature itself.

The large-span glass exterior of the Great Glass House at the National Botanical Garden of Wales (by Foster and Partners and Anthony Hunt Associates) is a good example of the new three-dimensional possibilities. It is based on the shape of a tyre's inner tube. Although the roof is a curving glass form, the shape of the individual panels repeats to aid production. The final effect is as much inspired by the surrounding soft rolling countryside as by the structural demands of its 99 x 55 m (325 x 180 ft) span. As if to continue the topographical illusion, only the gently curving glass roof is visible as the rest of the building sinks underground.

The advantages plastics have over glass are weight and strength, resulting in a lighter and potentially more transparent enclosure, but with the problems described earlier. However, a relatively new material invented in the 1960s has given architects an exciting opportunity to make incredibly

International Terminal,
Waterloo Station

Nicholas Grimshaw & Partners,
1993

lightweight transparent buildings. It is called Ethylene Tetrafluoroethylene foil (ETFE).

And so to Eden

ETFE was the essential ingredient for the biomes at Eden. It is more transparent than glass, as ultraviolet light can pass through it, and to an extent allows the concepts of Buckminster Fuller to be fully realized; it can span up to six or seven times the distance of glass between supports when used for a roof. Creating an architectural form that would make full use of the properties of ETFE foil was one of our driving influences for the Eden biome designs.

I have already touched upon the undeniable connection between glasshouse technology and railway halls. In 1993 we completed the Waterloo International Terminal in London. There had been little new railway architecture in the UK since the nineteenth century, so the terminal symbolized not only a renaissance of high-speed rail travel, but also a permanent gateway to mainland Europe. The high-impact snaking glass roof (which used only 10% of the overall building budget) is its most striking feature, and the emblem of this new service.

The technical challenge for Grimshaw was to design a roof structure and envelope that could follow the twisting and diminishing geometry of the tracks. This was the first project that we designed in three dimensions on the computer. For speed and economy, the glazing had to use standard rectilinear sheets of glass. In collaboration with Anthony Hunt Associates we developed a steel and glass roof that took on the sinuous shape of the tracks below, using the glass as overlapping sheets rather like scales on a snake. This loose skin connected back to the steel skeleton through a series of adjustable connectors.

The great railway halls of the nineteenth century had been greatly influenced by the technological developments of the earlier glasshouses. These heroic railway structures were a great inspiration for our work at Waterloo and so the story goes full circle, as it was this structure that prompted the invitation to prepare proposals for the then undeveloped Cornwall Eden Project site. In the summer of 1995 I met Tim Smit, Jonathan Ball and Ronnie Murning from Eden. We walked around the roof of Waterloo and discussed how it could inspire a fresh approach to glasshouse design for a new type of botanical garden. The final fruits of those discussions illustrate this book.

Architects
Nicholas Grimshaw & Partners

Jason Ahmed
Vanessa Bartulovic
Dean Boston
Jolyon Brewis
Chris Brieger
Matt Bugg
Antje Bulthaup
Vincent Chang
Julian Coward
Amanda Davis
Mat Eastwood
Florian Eckhardt
Nick Grimshaw
Malgorzata Haley
Alex Haw
Ben Heath
David Hebblethwaite
Bill Horgan
Perry Hooper
David Kirkland
Oliver Konrath
Angelika Kovacic
Melissa Lim
Su Ling Tan
Declan McCafferty
Richard Morrell
Charles Meloy
Diane Murdoch
Tim Narey
Monica Niggemeyer
Killian O'Sullivan
Michael Pawlyn
Deborah Penn
Martin Pirnie
Simon Platt
Juan Porral-Hermida
Wenke Reitz-Lykouria
Mustafa Salman
Jerry Tate
Andy Thomas
Olivia Weston
Andrew Whalley

Structural Engineer
Anthony Hunt Associates

Services Engineer
Arup (Visitor Centre and biomes)
BDSP Partnership
    (Foundation Building)
Buro Happold (Dry Tropics Biome
    and Education Centre)

**Project Manager and Cost
Consultant**
Davis Langdon & Everest

Project Supervisor
Land Architects (Visitor Centre
    and biomes)
Haskoll (Foundation Building)
Scott Wilson (Dry Tropics Biome
    and Education Centre)

Planning Supervisor
Waterman Burrow Crocker

Landscape
Land Use Consultants

Fire Consultant
Arup Fire

Cladding Consultant
Arup Façade Engineering

Main Contractor
Sir Robert McAlpine/
    Alfred McAlpine Construction
    Joint Venture

Steelwork Contractor
Mero UK plc (biomes)

ETFE Sub-Contractor
Foiltec/Vector Special Projects

Transworld Publishers
61–63 Uxbridge Road,
London W5 5SA
a division of The Random House Group Ltd

Random House Australia (PTY) Ltd
20 Alfred Street, Milsons Point,
Sydney, New South Wales 2061,
Australia

Random House New Zealand Ltd
18 Poland Road, Glenfield,
Auckland 10, New Zealand

Random House South Africa (PTY) Ltd
Endulini, 5a Jubilee Road,
Parktown 2193, South Africa

Published 2003 by Eden Project Books
a division of Transworld Publishers

Copyright 'This Other Eden'
© Hugh Pearman 2003

Copyright 'Eden and the Glasshouse
Tradition'
© Andrew Whalley 2003

Designed and typeset by
Isambard Thomas, London

Managing Editor: Emma Callery

Printed in China
by C & C Offset Printing Co. Ltd

1 3 5 7 9 10 8 6 4 2

Papers used by Eden Project Books
are natural, recyclable products
made from wood grown in sustainable
forests. The manufacturing processes
conform to the environmental
regulations of the country of origin.

www.booksattransworld.co.uk

Photograph acknowledgements

The publishers would like to thank
the following photographers for their
permission to use their pictures.

Arcaid/Richard Bryant: p.108

Corbis/Bettman: p.115

Peter Cook/VIEW: pp.36–7, 72, 73, 75,
82–3, 88, 90–1, 92, 93, 94, 95, 117

Devonshire Collection, Chatsworth.
By permission of the Duke of Devonshire
and the Chatsworth Settlement Trustees:
p.107

Simon Doling: p.25 bottom left, right

Michael Dyer Associates: pp.18 top left,
right, bottom left, 21 top left, right, 102

Charles Francis: pp.22, 25 top, 26

Chris Gascoigne/VIEW: p.100

Perry Hooper: p.119

Herbie Knott: pp.2–3, 27, 30, 38–9,
48–9

Red Cover/Hugh Palmer: p.105

Edmund Sumner: pp.40–1, 42–3, 44–5,
46–7, 50–1, 52, 53, 62–3, 64, 65, 66,
67, 68, 70, 71, 74, 76–8, 80–1, 84–5,
86–7, 97, 98, 99

Topham Picturepoint/The British Library:
p.111

Tessa Traeger: pp.10–12, 13, 54–6, 57,
58, 59, 60–1

Andrew Whalley: p.112

www.smoothe.co.uk: p.29